THE AUTHORITY GUIDE TO
PRACTICAL
MINDFULNESS

How to improve your productivity, creativity and
focus by slowing down for just 10 minutes a day

TOM EVANS

The Authority Guide to Practical Mindfulness
How to improve your productivity, creativity and focus by slowing down for
just ten minutes a day
© Tom Evans

ISBN 978-1-909116-73-3
eISBN 978-1-909116-74-0

Published in 2016 by Authority Guides
authorityguides.co.uk

The right of Tom Evans to be identified as the author
of this work has been asserted by him in accordance with the
Copyright, Designs and Patents Act 1988.

A CIP record of this book is available from the British Library.

No responsibility for loss occasioned to any person acting or
refraining from action as a result of any material in this publication
can be accepted by the author or publisher.

Printed in the United Kingdom.

To Louise for giving me time and space.

Acknowledgements

As with all projects, this series of books would not happen if it wasn't for seeds and assistance provided by other people.

Thanks to Sue Richardson for popping along, just in time. Thanks to the PR authority who is Chantal Cooke for reconnecting me with Sue.

To the wonderful souls at Insight Timer with whom I am playing a small role helping to get the whole world meditating, one person at a time.

To the team at the Impact Foundation, with whom I am helping to restore sight to people in the developing world with donations from meditators in the developed world. This is an example of practical mindfulness in commercial action.

Thanks to Barbara Eastman, Mark Hobin, Kelly Mundt and Maria Waite for beautifying my draft manuscript.

Contents

Just as you wouldn't leave the house without taking a shower, you shouldn't start the day without at least 10 minutes of meditation.

Marianne Williamson

Starting: the best time to plant a tree is yesterday

All journeys have secret destinations of which the traveler is unaware.

Martin Buber

Starting: the best time to plant a tree is yesterday

All journeys start somewhere and end somewhere else. Along the way, some experiences are had, learnings acquired and new vistas seen.

People who start a mindfulness meditation journey all start in different places. Some get stressed and burnt out by the pressures of corporate life. Some suffer from anxiety and depression. Some experience a traumatic life event and need respite and healing. Some want to find their place in the grand scheme of things and seek spiritual enlightenment.

My introduction to meditation began because of the first of these reasons. In my early 40s, I was heading up a creative team delivering ecommerce solutions. They had discovered I was reasonably good at sales after I had had a stupendous first year where I secured over £1m of business. So, in year two, I was given an expanded team to manage to deliver on projects secured in the first year of sales and, at the same time, given a sales target that had doubled. Even with my high work ethic and energy, it all proved to be too much for me. I only made it half-way through year three before I threw in the towel. For the first time in my life, I left a job without one to go to. Up to this point, I had fallen from fabulous opportunity into fabulous opportunity.

I wouldn't exactly call this a mid-life crisis; it was rather more of a mid-life hiccup. I was, and still am, a pretty resilient and optimistic chap and I knew I would bounce back and that, as Mr Micawber would say, 'Something will turn up.'

While I was still struggling in what turned out to be my last corporate role, I did look pretty haggard and someone suggested I should meditate. At the time, I should add, the term 'mindfulness' was not in common circulation as it is today. My first reaction to this suggestion was that I was far too busy to waste 10 to 20 minutes a day. My second reaction was that there would be no way I could make my overactive mind go quiet. I persisted though and discovered some simple techniques that helped me to get easily and repeatedly into the meditative state. Regular practice ended up opening up many new vistas and opportunities, which have led to me writing this book some 15 years later.

I quickly discovered that meditation certainly reduced my stress and anxiety and, on reflection, probably lead to me having the bravery to leave that highly stressful job. I quickly discovered that the daily practice of meditation started to produce many tangible, real-world outcomes that I found could be used for business, as well as personal benefit. When I first left university, I got a job as a BBC TV engineer and had been fascinated by the magic of television. After learning to meditate, I became fascinated by the magic of the mind and went on a journey to research the nature of consciousness.

As a result of what I have learned, it is my aim that this book gives you a new and different motivation to embrace the practice of mindfulness meditation. You will discover that it is the key to a more successful and rewarding life and an easier way to run a more profitable business. Just imagine a world where opportunity turns up at your door. Imagine clients just finding you and, as a result, giving you more time to work on other aspects of your business. Imagine invention and innovation oozing out of your pores, and creativity in all aspects of your business abounding. Imagine a happier workplace, with reduced negativity and gossip around the water cooler. Imagine productivity improvements from a more motivated team. Imagine a full order book and a queue of people wanting to come and work with you.

So when we make a new start to a new way of being, it's a good idea to stop something else. In this book, I encourage you to take at least ten minutes of 'me time' every day. To create space for this to happen, have a think about what you can stop doing. Changing an unwanted habit for a habit you do want is the secret to all successful personal development.

The journey ahead

So this guide to practical mindfulness describes a journey where I explain what mindfulness is, and isn't, and how it can be accessed by entering the meditative state. I will then explain how to use mindfulness meditation to enhance your business and take it to places that may be currently unimaginable.

- On this journey, you will discover how to relax, improve your wellbeing and increase your vitality.
- As we are naturally inefficient, you will learn the secrets of staying focused to counteract this tendency.
- We will explore how we get in the zone and allow the two halves of our brain to work in harmony.

- You will discover how to generate ideas 'off the top of your head'.
- You will learn how to create more time.
- You will find out how to get opportunities and clients to turn up at your door with little or no effort.
- You will learn how to be mindful in group environments and reduce meeting times.
- You will discover how to get teams to work better together, to play to their strengths and to think and act together.
- We explore how to love the work you do, and people you do it with, so you never have to 'work' as such again.

To take this journey, there is no need to convert your boardroom into a shrine, or to get the whole workforce meditating for an hour at the start of every day. Certainly, it would be great if everyone did take some individual 'me time', but this type of journey is one of personal choice. It's not about joining or forming a cult. When you embrace the principles of practical mindfulness, you will achieve a new type of commercial success and, at the same time, you will benefit personally. You can also be the only person in your company working in this way and you will find your increase in vitality is what I call 'nicely infectious'. People might ask if you have had cosmetic surgery when they notice the lines of worry fall from your face. They may notice how you seem to always land on your feet, while all around you is chaos.

This journey is not one of asceticism, becoming vegan, giving all your possessions away, or changing your creed and becoming a Buddhist. You may of course harbour a desire to become more philanthropic with your enterprise. With more time on your hands and with an increase in profitability in your business, these are potential opportunities that may open up for you.

Slow and steady

This is one of those journeys where slow and steady wins the race. Just taking 10 to 20 minutes out a day is the only investment needed. The return on your investment will come very quickly, as you will soon find yourself experiencing the benefits of smoother-running days when you take 'me time' each day.

After just a few weeks, you will begin to get medium-term return on your investment in 'me time', as you become more creative, luckier, more productive and happier in what you are doing.

There is a long-term return on investment to be had, too. Many scientific studies have confirmed that regular meditation reduces the ravages of time and delays the onset of diseases that plague so many in their later years. It has been claimed that every single minute you meditate increases your longevity in proportion. As it improves your general wellbeing, it gives you the ability to live better and more healthily for longer.

With such benefits to be had in the short, medium and long terms, the sooner we start, the sooner we benefit.

How to embrace this book

As this is a practical guide to mindfulness, a great way to embrace the ideas in this book is to actually experience them. So each chapter is accompanied by a ten minute guided visualisation that will help you to enter and experience the meditative state. For purchasers of the print or e-reader versions of the book, just go to www.tomevans.co/tag2pm to get complimentary access. You will also discover how I am applying the principles of practical mindfulness philanthropically.

There are two ways to read this book. You can read it all the way through and come back and listen to the meditations in your own time. Alternatively, you can take your time and take in a chapter and then listen to its companion meditation. Although it's a book that can be read in one sitting, or a couple of commutes, you might like to take in a chapter and a meditation a day at a time. As you will see, slowing down is the new speeding up.

The guided visualisations are all exactly ten minutes long and are nicely addictive. If you are going to have one habit, ten minutes of chill-out time just for yourself each day is a habit with nothing but positive side effects.

Here's some general guidelines for the visualisations:

- Ensure you have ten uninterruptible minutes set aside each day
- They are best listened to on headphones
- You can listen to them at any time of the day
- You can sit upright or lie down
- It doesn't matter if you fall asleep
- It's not a good idea to listen to them while driving.

Just for Today

The first visualisation is called Just for Today. The way we start a day has a big effect on how the day as a whole pans out. This is why ten minutes of mindfulness meditation at the start of each day has such a beneficial effect. This first visualisation sets each and every day off with the most amazing start. Use it daily if you like, starting from now. So take a ten minute pause right now and listen to the first visualisation.

Key takeaways

All journeys require taking a first step.

Mindfulness is an exploration not a destination.

Slow and steady wins the race.

The starting point of discovering who you are, your gifts, your talents, your dreams, is being comfortable with yourself.

Robin S. Sharma

Relaxing: making your days run smoothly

Your mind will answer most questions if
you learn to relax and wait for the answer.

William S. Burroughs

Relaxing: making your days run smoothly

By and large, the way we start our day sets the tone for the rest of the day. Start out stressed and your day will be stressful. Begin the day in a relaxed manner and you will find that your day will run much more smoothly. What's more, when we are relaxed, people around us are relaxed too and we create relaxing surroundings that are pleasant to be in.

This is what I discovered when I first started meditating in my mid-40s. I found that giving myself just ten minutes of 'me time' each day was all it took. On days when I couldn't do this first thing, I would at least go for a walk in a park near where I worked at lunchtime. I found that I got the time I invested back easily in time savings during the day. My productivity, focus and creativity all increased. Since then, I have learned that keeping up with regular meditation over a number of years also promotes good health and vitality. I look less haggard now than I did ten years ago. When we meditate over a prolonged period of time, we live more healthily for longer and we get the time we invest back in spades. So, in many ways, it's a kind of madness not to meditate.

Being mindful about mindfulness

Now this is a book on practical mindfulness, not so much practical meditation. So it's worth sorting out any confusion between the terms 'mindfulness' and 'meditation' and the phrase 'mindfulness meditation'.

There is, perhaps, some confusion that mindfulness means meditation – and that meditation means mindfulness. Let me state from the outset, you can be mindful without meditating and meditate without being mindful. This confusion is, perhaps, understandable, as learning to meditate is the most common route to achieving a mindful state of being. As mindfulness has its roots in Buddhist philosophy, it is natural that meditation plays such a big role.

To confuse things a little further, one of the meditative techniques used to teach mindfulness is to empty the mind of all thought. So, in some respects, being 'mind-full' involves being somewhat 'mind-less'. The words 'mindless' and 'mindlessness', however, bring up all sorts of connotations we want to avoid.

In the Buddhist tradition, mindfulness is the practice of bringing the attention to the internal and external experiences occurring in the present moment. Meditation is the mechanism used to still the mind so we can focus and channel the attention. Mindfulness meditation is a blanket term, then, to describe what happens when we do both together.

Some people worry whether they are 'doing it right' and somewhat ironically can become quite stressed by the process of learning and practising meditation. Certainly, there are some deep and elevated states of consciousness open to us all, but there is no concept of right or wrong when it comes to meditating. We are all natural meditators anyway. If you have ever driven on a familiar route and don't quite remember getting from A to B, you fell into a light meditative state. You can do the same painting a fence, mowing the lawn, ironing or washing the dishes. We are hard-wired to meditate.

My approach to meditation is somewhat more relaxed than some traditional, formal schools. With this book, the concepts are introduced gently, along with practical examples of how to use them. Some people will gain benefit from just being more at peace and relaxed. Some may well experience altered states of consciousness that they may interpret as mystical experiences. This is all quite normal and, as a scientist who has studied metaphysics, all quite explainable.

If you are a couch potato and want to run a marathon, you start jogging first, gently mixing your running with some walking. Gradually you build up and up. The same is true of meditation. In time, you can learn to stay in the meditative state with your eyes open and jump into a state I call EMT – or Extended Me Time. Here time elongates so we get more done with less of it. I can personally attest it works a treat for all creative tasks, like writing a book like this one.

Methods of meditation

A bit like riding a bike, once you learn to meditate, you can enter the meditative state on demand. Also like riding a bike, if you have to think about balancing on two wheels, you would fall off. The reason for this leads us to understand how we can enter the meditative state easily, consciously and on demand.

The normal human mind is only capable of having one thought at a time. If we think about the content of a thought, we lose its direction. If we think about the direction of a thought, we lose its content. Just think about this notion for a while to see what I mean.

I should say, in passing, that there is nothing 'normal' about the human mind and, with a little training, it is possible to run concurrent thought streams.

So this singular nature of thought is the basis for the most common meditative techniques (Figure 1). When we replace our inner chatter with another thought, the inner conversation has no option but to go quiet. After a while, it gives up and our thoughts basically 'disappear'. Incidentally, when we do this, time takes on a different quality too.

Figure 1 Methods of meditation

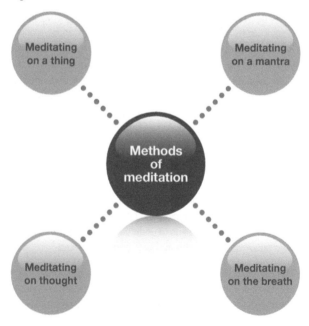

Meditating on a mantra

So, the most common technique is the repetition of a mantra (or saying). This is the method popularised on film and TV, as observing silent meditation is like watching paint dry. Mantras can be 'recited' out loud or 'in loud'. Repetition of a prayer or responses to a clergyman, rabbi or imam have a similar effect.

By way of example, just repeat these words in your head seven times. Say, 'just' on the in breath and 'relax' on the out breath. If you find that you lose count, it's working, as repeating the mantra and counting both need our brain. One way around this, not that it's important, but by way of example, is to use your fingers to do the counting and your mind to chant the mantra. Try it to see the effect.

Meditating on the breath

Another common method of meditation is to use the breath. We simply focus on the in breath and then the out breath and sometimes on the 'still point' between the in and out breaths. There are many variations on the depth, length and source of the breath too. The breath can come physically through the mouth or nostrils and metaphysically from places like the base of our spine and top of our head. We can breathe from our belly and through our heart, too. Experimentation is part of the game.

A simple breathing technique to try is the Haa breath. This involves breathing in through the nostrils, and then breathing out with a slightly open mouth making an 'haaaaah' sound. The accompanying visualisation for this chapter, called Just Breathe, will introduce you to meditations on a mantra and on the breath.

Meditating on thought

A deeper level of meditation is attainable from meditating on thought itself. Often, meditating on the breath first is used to ease into this state. When we begin to meditate on a thought, the thought we are observing has no option but to disappear. What follows is known as the 'collapse of thought'. It is from this state that we can allow light bulb moments to arrive.

The visualisation that accompanies the next chapter on focusing, called Just a Thought, will show you how to do this.

Meditating on a thing

You can get the hang of meditating with your eyes open by meditating on an object. Classically, a candle flame is used, but you can as easily just pick a spot on the wall. You both observe the object and, alternately, everything around the object. As you do so, the act of observation allows your mind to wander, and perhaps to wonder.

By continually coming back to the object of your focus, and defocusing your eyes, the mind eventually goes blank. The visualisation that accompanies the chapter on creating, called Just Musing, will show you how to do this.

Modes of mindfulness

While there is no need to become a practising Buddhist to benefit from mindfulness meditation, some of the tenets of Buddhist philosophy are immensely practical, and useful in business, so worth exploring here. For the avoidance of any doubt, I should state that I am neither a Buddhist nor, for that matter, an 'Anything-ist'. As I said, there is no need to join a cult or change your faith to benefit from the practice of, and practical outcomes from, mindfulness meditation.

In Buddhism, there are four 'modes of mindfulness' (Figure 2). These modes are all worth 'bearing in mind' for anyone who wants to be successful in business, and life.

Figure 2 Modes of mindfulness

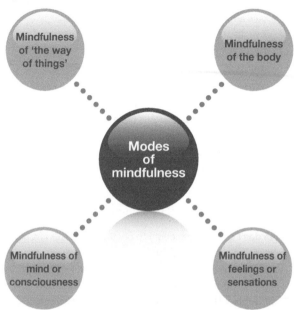

Modes of mindfulness

Mindfulness of the body

If we are mindful of our body, we notice what it is telling us.
Symptoms such as irritable bowel syndrome are a sure sign
we are stressed. Heart disease is often seeded by not being
loved or appreciated, or not loving what we do and who we
are with. Ankle, knee and hip pain can come from the fear of
stepping forward. Back and neck pain can be seeded from
us carrying too heavy a burden. Our body is the vehicle that

carries us around and nagging and persistent low-level ill-nesses are a sign we need to pull in for a pit stop.

Mindfulness of feelings or sensations

It pays great dividends to become mindful of our feelings. As you will see, our gut and heart centres are now recognised by neurologists as 'intelligences' that interact continually with the mind that sits in our brain. Ignore their advice at your peril. Unlike our brain, they don't 'speak' in a language and their messages often get swamped by our loud internal dialogue. As you listen to the meditations in this book, you will find you will be able to tune into them with ease.

Mindfulness of mind or consciousness

We don't give much thought to our thoughts. This is a great shame as, what we are thinking, fundamentally creates the world around us. On one level, this is subjective, for example whether we see our glass as half full or half empty. On a whole other level, it is because thoughts don't so much be-come things but are things. When you practise meditation for just a few weeks, you will find that what you think starts to manifest in your world. Now this may be not so much that you are creating your reality from your thoughts, but you just become better at noticing opportunities – or some mix of both of these.

Mindfulness of 'the way of things'

The saying that 'what goes around comes around' is one of those maxims that holds universally true. It is a truism that sits somewhat beyond religion, faith and scientific analysis. We 'know' it is true because it seems to work. If we are kind to people, they are kind in return. In business, I find if I pay all my suppliers promptly, I get paid quickly too. If you deliver on time, or always slightly over-deliver, you will find others will respond 'in kind'. If someone ever falls foul of this 'way of things', it pays dividends to be mindful as to why they have done so. It may be a sign that they need help or guidance or that there is something we can do to improve ourselves and our communication with that person.

Time to relax

While some people's idea of relaxation might be retiring to the Caribbean and sitting on a beach sipping cocktails all day, most people live in a reality that is somewhat different. Many have kids to get to school, and some kids are facing exams and being told what to do by parents and teachers. Some people will get stressed out by their boss and some bosses will get stressed out by employees. Some won't have any work, income or a roof over their heads while some might have a roof that needs repairing, but may not have the money to pay the bill.

When people aren't so relaxed, it can therefore be a bit stressful if someone comes along and tells them to take a chill pill, to snap out of it and not to worry as 'something will turn up'. If this sounds like you, you may also feel that taking ten minutes out each day to relax will just add to your stress. If this is the case, the way to approach meditation and mindfulness is to see it initially as a respite that will give you some release from the pressure of life for a few minutes a day.

After just a few weeks, or days, of practice you will see the world around you in a new light. What was at first a chore becomes a habit and what was once a habit becomes a way to be. Take it on trust that you will get the time back many times over.

Just Breathe

So before reading the next chapter, continue your mindfulness journey by listening to Just Breathe. This visualisation introduces the most basic and simple meditative techniques that use the breath and what is known as a mantra. You might like to lie down and relax to this one and it doesn't matter if you drift off to sleep. You will not be 'doing it wrong', it is just being mindful of what your body needs.

Key takeaways

When we are relaxed, our lives flow much more smoothly.

Meditation is a natural state that helps us become more mindful.

There are four main methods to enter the meditative state.

There are also four modes of mindfulness.

We get the time we invest in meditation back easily.

Focusing: the retention of your attention

Focus on the journey, not the destination.
Joy is found not in finishing an activity but
in doing it.

Greg Anderson

Focusing: the retention of your attention

Using the breath as an object to 'focus' upon is one of the simplest meditative techniques available to us.

If during the day, something makes your blood boil, just take three to five deep in and out breaths before you respond. Focus on the in breath, focus on the out breath and focus on the gaps between the in and the out breaths. When we take a few breaths before reacting, we can both take time to consider our reaction and to reflect on what has made us so angry in the first place. Taking 'a breather' is a fabulous natural tonic and there are some beneficial side effects to deeper breathing too. We better oxygenate our cells and our neurology and help to remove toxins from our body. Diaphragmatic breathing releases serotonin into our bloodstream, which is a neurotransmitter that helps to stabilise our moods.

We tend not to give much thought to our thoughts and why, for example, we can switch from being calm to livid in less than a second. From when we awaken until when we fall asleep, something remarkable happens each day that we take for granted. We start to think. This self-propelled biological machine, which is you and I, and is comprised of trillions of cells, can not only observe the world around it, but can also reflect and muse on the fact it has the ability to do this. I am doing that right now as I write this, as are you as you read this.

Why we are 10 per cent efficient

What we also don't tend to give much thought to is why and how our internal commentary starts up all by itself and not only runs all day but also, in some people, runs their day. Each second of each waking day, most people are entrenched in thought. Some will be thinking out loud, that is talking, but most will be thinking 'in loud'.

Now and again, an 'in loud' thought can escape unintentionally. When we encounter someone suffering from disease of the mind, or dementia, often what is going on inside their heads is clear to see or hear.

In most cases, we will either be focusing on a task in hand or our thoughts will wander. We might think about what we are having for supper or rehearse a speech or impending conversation with our boss. We might be reflecting on a fabulous weekend we've just had or replaying a conversation that didn't go too well.

Our train of thought also tends to get disrupted. The phone might ring. An email might ping in. Or we might think it's time to have a cup of coffee.

Our minds seem predisposed not only to wonder but also to wander. Figure 3 shows how most people are naturally around 10 per cent efficient.

Figure 3 Typical waking thoughts

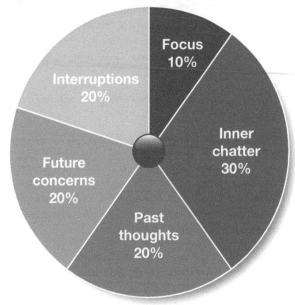

As we will explore in more depth later, it is a misconception that all thoughts emanate from our heads. Our brains are as much a receiver of thought as they are generators of thought forms. When I studied electronic engineering, I learned how early telegraphs, and even some early modems, could either transmit or receive, but not do both at the same time. For all their magical sophistication, our brains are like this, too. It is nearly impossible to listen to another conversation if we are talking out loud. Similarly, if we are thinking, then we cannot receive thoughts. You can also try handwriting and thinking at the same time to experience this phenomenon. You will find you have to think about what you want to write and then write it. If thoughts come in, you stop writing.

Mindfalls

This is where practising mindfulness meditation comes in. It helps us form a new relationship with our thoughts. We should be mindful that our brain receives external thoughts from three main sources.

The first is via our senses. What we see, hear and feel modulates our thoughts.

Second, we take inputs from other parts of our neurology, which come to us in the form of feelings, such as instincts, intuitions, hunger and being in love or unloved.

The third input is flashes of inspiration and enlightenment. These often pop in unannounced and unexpectedly, sometimes while out walking, or when in the shower.

Some thoughts can take over our mind and we can enter what is known as a 'mindfall'. If you get awoken in the early hours with a brilliant idea, it can be impossible to go back to sleep as you run through all the ramifications. If somebody oversteps the mark or crosses a boundary, thoughts of righting that wrong can consume our waking days. If you fall either in or out of love, creativity can fly out of the window. In this case, not only are you in a mindfall but a 'heartfall' too.

Mindfalls are also contagious. If an employee is enraged about something at work, they can share their anger and wind up their colleagues. Their anger can even spread to customers and suppliers. If an employee is excited about an idea or invention, their passion can also spread like wildfire. This can be either detrimental or beneficial depending on the circumstances. When it comes to mindfalls, we have to be mindful of when we are in one.

Thinking about thoughts

Many people who take up meditation feel they are doing it incorrectly because thoughts pop along while they are supposed to be meditating. Meditation is not about having no thoughts at all, but just in forming new relationships with our thoughts and with our feelings. These are two of the modes of mindfulness.

If we do find ourselves in a mindfall, the easiest escape is to resort to our breath. Either just take a few deep in and out breaths, or even take ten minutes out to cool down and listen to the Just Breathe visualisation again. When we have suffered from a transgression, thoughts of revenge can easily surface and take over our mind. We become enslaved by our own thoughts and entrapped in our mindfalls.

The singular nature of thought, which can make us inefficient, is the key to freeing ourselves from thoughts that go round and round in our heads. If we talk to a thought, it stops it dead in its tracks. We can ask the thought, or ourselves, why we are experiencing that thought in the first place. Let's say someone made us angry, we can ask what exactly we are so angry about. We can ask if it is that person's actions or words or our reaction to them that we are really angry about. We can ask those thoughts of anger to go away as we are busy and tell them that we will deal with them later.

Often when we do this, the source of our anger abates when we realise it's only our reaction causing the distress. By not reacting, and by remaining detached, we can elevate ourselves above the emotion of anger. We might replace it with compassion and empathy or do something even more enlightened still. Just imagine if the behaviour that causes the reaction in you might also afflict others. You could take your experience at learning how to control your rage and teach others to do the same. When we become creative about adversity and negativity, we transmute it into opportunity by flooding it with positivity. We have become truly mindful about our thoughts.

Asking for guidance

When we start to tune into our thoughts, a whole new world opens up for us. We can ask for guidance and direction, and answers and help will just show up. With the ubiquity of social media, we can encapsulate our question in a tweet, or perform a Wikipedia or Google search and be rewarded with just the information we need, at the perfect time. When we practise mindfulness meditation, we can get the answer just with our mind alone.

We can occasionally over-think a situation or a problem and find it impossible to see the 'wood for the trees'. By becoming relaxed about it and just going for that walk or meditating, the solution has the tendency to pop in 'out of nowhere'. By defocusing, we end up zooming in and focusing on exactly what we need.

It is worth being mindful of the four modes of mindfulness here. The answer might well come in as a thought but it may just be a feeling or a sight, a sound or even a smell. It also may come in the form of a sign, a metaphor or even in a dream. It may come in the form of an insight or a life lesson.

If we really don't get the answer, there are two possibilities. First, our minds and our lives may be too busy to spot it. Second, we could do with asking a different, or better, question.

Changing perspectives

It is natural that we tend to see the world from our own perspective, as we perceive it through our senses of sight, sound, feeling, taste and smell. As our senses and sense of self are so strong and pervasive, it can be sometimes difficult to see things in perspective.

While our senses inform us about the world, it is our thoughts that inform us as to what we think and feel about it. For example, we might think that one thing about our business, products or services is not that great, but our customers might see it in a completely different light. We may see our competitors being more successful than us, yet they might yearn for a quality, or skill, that they see in us.

We can use the modes of mindfulness to gain insight into both the internal and external parts of our business.

- We can be mindful of the 'body' and component parts of our business. Is it healthy? Are all the parts of the business working in harmony?

- We can be mindful about what we feel about it. Do we love working there? Do we admire what the business represents and how it carries itself?

- We can be mindful of the 'mind' of the business. Is it inspiring? Is it leading and innovating? Does it have a vision of where it is going?

- We can be mindful about how well it fits in with the 'way of things'. Is it fair to its employees and its supply chain? Does it hold the customers' best interests at heart?

On the surface, this might sound like somewhat of a nebulous way to think about a business. We are, after all, not analysing the profit and loss, balance sheet or order book. By changing perspective to a more abstract level, we become able to understand how aspects of a business that are not going well come about. We can also celebrate and pat ourselves on the back for what is working well.

Often a small change in how we think about our business, and ourselves, is all that is needed to make a change. This level of abstraction can allow us to see that all our problems are seeded by one or two fundamental issues that we really need to address. We might not be talking to customers enough. One department might not be communicating well with another. Maybe we should increase our prices and share the wealth by paying our suppliers a little more. If this latter idea is a little naive, by creating more value in our proposition, our customers could be happier to 'invest' a little more in what we have to offer.

It all comes down to a matter of perspective and how we think and feel.

Just a Thought

Before reading the next chapter, continue your mindfulness journey by listening to Just a Thought. Thinking about our thinking is a bit like changing a tyre while we are travelling at speed down the fast lane of a motorway. As our thoughts start up automatically without us having to 'reboot our system' every morning, it is difficult to switch them off while we are awake. Well, this visualisation will show you how you can do exactly that. As you heard in the very first visualisation, it gives you the ability to put distance between your thoughts and your mood.

Key takeaways

We are hard-wired to experience one thought at a time.

If our attention drifts, our efficiency drops.

When thoughts rage around our heads, we enter a mindfall.

Help is always at hand if we only ask.

A change of perspective is a breath of fresh air.

Creating: why two brains are better than one

The role of a creative leader is not to have all the ideas; it's to create a culture where everyone can have ideas and feel that they're valued.

Ken Robinson

Creating: why two brains are better than one

In order to understand how to use mindfulness techniques in the creative process, we have to switch our focus to areas of our neurology only usually probed by magnetic resonance imaging (MRI) scanners.

Back in the 1960s, a pioneering neurosurgeon, Professor Roger Sperry, was amongst the first researchers to discover that our brains exhibited asymmetry. He won a Nobel Prize for his research. As a result of his research, the urban myth sneaked into consciousness and culture that the left brain was logical and the right brain creative. This is now known to be a gross oversimplification. The discovery that the right side of our body was primarily mapped to the left hemisphere, and vice versa, was correct though.

At the time, most brain research was carried out on patients who had experienced some kind of trauma, such as a stroke or physical brain damage. These days, scanners can look inside the brains of healthy people, and parts of their brain can be temporarily disrupted from performing normally. The person can then describe how they feel and what they are thinking and experiencing.

It turns out that the left and right hemispheres do undertake different tasks. More specifically, they undertake similar tasks differently. In general, the right brain looks at the whole and embraces the new. The left brain handles detail and processes learned responses. Note that even this is also a generalisation and vast oversimplification.

Here's an example of how it works. When a chicken is pecking the ground for seeds, its right eye (which is wired to its left brain) looks at the ground while the left eye (wired to its right brain) scans for predators. For more on all of this, read the excellent book by Ian McGilchrist (Yale University Press, 2009) called *The Master and His Emissary*. You may well ask, what has how a chicken feeds got to do with our creativity and mindfulness in general?

In two minds

In the last chapter, we explored how we can create and change perspective by forming a new relationship with our thoughts, especially once we appreciate their singular nature.

We can become even more mind-full of how we operate when we embrace the notion that we are blessed with two minds that experience the world in different ways. This becomes even more insight-full when we learn that these two minds experience the passage of time differently, too. Note that the hyphens are intentional in this paragraph.

Our two hemispheres are connected together via a butterfly-shaped structure in the centre of our brain known as the corpus callosum. Sperry discovered that he could calm epileptics down by severing it completely. This was a great and inspired discovery at the time, but one that perhaps would have not been as necessary had they been taught to meditate on their thoughts.

One of Sperry's most significant discoveries was that both hemispheres could operate independently of each other and that one half of our brain can be conscious and aware without the other side knowing what it is up to.

So we are blessed and equipped with two minds. Intuitively it will come as no surprise that we become supremely creative when both sides of the brain work on the same task at the same time, leaning to their respective strengths.

This is a mode known as whole brain thinking and we can access this state through mindfulness meditation and specific breathing techniques.

Not to be sniffed at

There is a specific breathing technique used in yoga called *Nadi Shodhan Pranayama*. Don't worry about remembering the name; I had to look it up. It involves breathing alternately through our right and left nostrils. With your mouth closed, you hold one nostril closed with your index finger and breathe through the other nostril say for three, five or seven breaths. You then flip over and breath through the other nostril. Try it now.

It should be noted that yoga means 'union' and this technique unifies the hemispheres of our brain. Note, though, that the practice of yoga itself unifies more than our hemispheres.

When we breathe through our right nostril, we energise our left hemisphere. Our right hemisphere is similarly energised through the left nostril. So this is a great exercise to do before embarking on a creative task, or if you find yourself flagging in the afternoon. If you are a teacher, you can use it to literally inspire a class.

Once both your hemispheres are energised, you become able to hold the detail of the task in mind (left brain) while simultaneously holding the whole vision (right brain). Each hemisphere gains an awareness of what the other is thinking. As you will discover, time also takes on an ethereal, elongated quality when we enter this state. This is the mythical zone where we tap into our creative flow.

Mapping your mind

Our brains do not think in lists, they think radially and by association. Thoughts course up, down and across neurons. If we played word association and I said 'cat', you may say 'dog', or 'cat flap'. If you said 'dog', I might say 'bark' and you might then say 'tree'. So we go from the notion of a cat to a tree in three steps. No computer can perform this feat in quite the same way, yet.

When it comes to problem solving and innovation, being mindsfull that this is how we are neurologically wired becomes incredibly useful.

When we then give our two minds something they can both do at the same time, they move up several gears in terms of their creative output. Any great work of art, such as an oil painting, a symphony or a novel, requires the artist to be a master of detail and of their craft while simultaneously holding the whole vision.

If you, like me and unlike Mozart, Van Gogh and Douglas Adams, are a mere mortal, we might need some help to pull off such brilliance. This is where the Mind Map, a brainchild of Tony Buzan, comes in handy. Before I write any book, I create a Mind Map of the chapter headings and the main themes they will cover. This allows my right brain to appreciate the book's overall structure while my left brain can focus on the detail. Mind

Maps allow us to freely associate around a central theme and, as such, give our imaginations free rein to play. They keep our left brain occupied with the detail while our right brain manages the whole vision.

'Aha, a map!' the left brain exclaims. 'I do the navigation around here.'

'Now the left brain is busy, I'll create a masterpiece,' the right brain whispers silently to itself.

Mind Maps are brilliant devices that we can use for shopping lists, planning and revision. As their structure maps pretty much directly on to our neurology, they are great for capturing the minutes of meetings or for planning a speech. Instead of taking copious notes on stage with you, a single sheet of paper is all that's needed on your lectern. We can use different colours, font types, images and icons to emphasise key points. They are much easier to commit to memory than a list.

By way of example, Figure 4 is what my right brain conjured up for my left brain to fill in the detail.

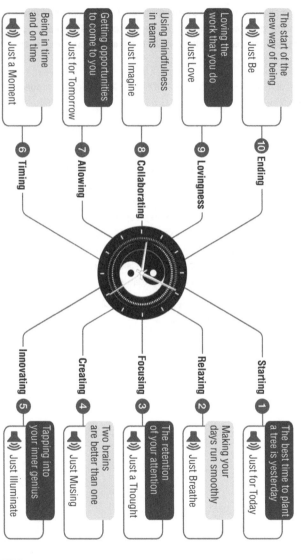

Figure 4 Mind Map of this book's structure

10 Ending
🔊 Just Be
The start of the new way of being

9 Lovingness
🔊 Just Love
Loving the work that you do

8 Collaborating
🔊 Just Imagine
Using mindfulness in teams

7 Allowing
🔊 Just for Tomorrow
Getting opportunities to come to you

6 Timing
🔊 Just a Moment
Being in time and on time

1 Starting
🔊 Just for Today
The best time to plant a tree is yesterday

2 Relaxing
🔊 Just Breathe
Making your days run smoothly

3 Focusing
🔊 Just a Thought
The retention of your attention

4 Creating
🔊 Just Musing
Two brains are better than one

5 Innovating
🔊 Just Illuminate
Tapping into your inner genius

40

Fuelling your creativity

Like all the cells in our body, our neurons need energy to operate. Neurons are fuelled by oxygen and glucose. The more challenging the brain's task is, the more fuel it consumes. The brain is only 2 per cent of our body weight, but it consumes about 20–25 per cent of its energy – around 25 watts. This is why the nostril breathing technique is so effective at literally inspiring us.

Our breath does more than keep us alive; it is brain fuel. This is one of the reasons why meditating on the breath is so beneficial. Most of the time, we breathe shallowly using just the intercostal muscles around our rib cage. When we use the diaphragm, we become in-spired.

We only need to breathe very deeply two or three times a day for a few in and out breaths to remain inspired for the whole day. It will come as no surprise that opera singers perform breathing exercises before a performance. Smart leaders who want to inspire at their annual general meetings can benefit from a few belly breaths before going on stage too.

It is worth being mindful that inspiration is powered by the in breath. We should also be mindful that our aspirations are delivered via the out breath. Inspiration and aspiration are the two halves of the respiration process.

Just Musing

This next visualisation will take you through a simple and repeatable technique to connect you with your muse and to get you into the zone before embarking on any creative task. You can also use this in a group environment, too.

Key takeaways

We all have at least two minds in our heads.

Our creativity soars when we use both brain hemispheres at the same time.

We can energise our hemispheres with alternate nostril breathing.

Mind Maps are whole brain devices.

The breath fuels the creative process.

Innovating: tapping into your inner genius

Exploration is the engine that drives innovation. Innovation drives economic growth. So let's all go exploring.

Edith Widder

Innovating: tapping into your inner genius

So you are now mindful that you possess two minds that experience the world in subtly different ways. What's more, they are literally inspired and fuelled by the breath and can be encouraged to work together, in concert and in harmony. When you prime the brain hemispheres with the breath, they become ready for action. All they need to get going is a spark.

We have all experienced flashes of brilliance and enlightenment in our life that changed our worlds, and our view of the world. For some, these flashes may come from watching TV or a film. Others might be inspired by a sunset, a book or a piece of music that transports them to another dimension.

Some well renowned geniuses, such as Newton, Da Vinci and Einstein, experienced moments of prescience – or pre-science – that changed our fundamental view of the universe. We also are fortunate to have modern day disruptive thinkers who change our world, such as Tim Berners-Lee, Steve Jobs and Elon Musk. They challenge convention and leave the world a different place by being here. Each of them experienced a spark, or three, and asked why it has to be as it is. They then did something about it and made something happen.

Ideas on tap

My favourite application for mindfulness meditation is how it opens the floodgates to an unlimited flow of ideas. So, when we still our mind, we become receptive to receiving such flashes of brilliance ourselves.

Now we might not have the mathematical ability of Stephen Hawking, to enable us to conjure up a new theory of everything. Each one of us, though, is only one meditation away from an idea that can transform our business, and perhaps will make us a million, if that is our thing. When we use the breath to prime our neurology and then still our mind by entering the meditative state, we become able to receive.

When we then experience a light bulb moment, we get the whole vision for an idea in less than a second. They occur inside time. If you were to scan the brain of someone who receives a light bulb moment, you would see large parts of both hemispheres light up momentarily. When a light bulb moment arrives, our right brain sees the whole vision in less than a second and our left brain is enraptured by the intricate detail, simplicity and beauty of the idea. They stop us in our tracks and are whole brain events.

Apocryphally, Archimedes had a 'eureka moment' in his bath when he worked out how to use the displacement of water to assay the quality of a gold crown. Isaac Newton experienced his 'aha moment' when he got the whole of the theory of gravity in less than a second. It's said that it took him the whole of the rest of his life to work out the mathematics.

If, at the time we experienced our moment of 'aha', our whole body was in an MRI scanner, we would see something rather larger unfold. Other areas of our neurology would also illuminate.

Light bulb moments are not only whole brain events but whole mind events. The reason they have such an effect on us is that they interact with our whole neurology. It is now known that our heart and gut have their own 'brains'. These mind centres are constantly interacting and informing the control centre and 'director of operations' in our head.

When the light bulb moment arrives, our heart falls in love with the idea and our gut gives it a green light. Our throat mind might even exclaim, 'Eureka!'

Decisions, decisions

When you learn how to generate light bulb moments on demand, rather than waiting for them to come along, you can get somewhat overwhelmed with ideas. As a result, it can be difficult to know which one to run with. At any one time, for example, I have four or five ideas milling around for my next book.

If you have ever said, 'My heart's not in it' or 'I wish I had trusted my gut on this or that', then you will have stumbled on the way to make the right decision every time. As mentioned, our heart and gut are active mind centres. When we get our head, heart and gut in alignment and agreement, we will rarely put a foot wrong.

Once you become more mindful about your thoughts, it is a small step to take to tune into what is essentially this natural inner guidance system. The first thing to bear in mind, when eliciting such responses, is that the gut and heart mind are old minds from an evolutionary perspective and don't possess language. Our gut will only give us a 'yes' or 'no' or a 'stop' or 'go' signal. Our heart 'speaks' in levels and so will be 'cold', 'lukewarm', 'hot' or 'positively boiling' about a perceived situation.

I mean the latter status in a good way, and not that you are fuming about something.

When seeking an answer to something that is imponderable, it is best to be specific in your question. So, for example, if I wanted to get my gut's advice on which of two books to write first, I cannot ask it if I should write Book A or Book B. I have to ask the two separate questions of, 'Should I write Book A next?' and 'Should I write Book B next?' If, by the way, I get two 'no's', then there probably is a Book C I should be writing. If I get two 'yes's', then perhaps Book A and Book B should be merged and refined in some way to produce Book C.

Making ideas actually happen

I am sure you've had a bright idea and done nothing with it. Then a year or so later, you see a product coming on the market exactly as you envisioned it and you kick yourself. In passing, one of the possible mechanisms that may explain how this happens is the postulation that we are all connected by a collective consciousness.

Anyhow, even though I am not a practising Buddhist, I do admire and use some of its methodologies and philosophies. One of them, called the Noble Eightfold Path, gives a very practical and useful framework to take an idea from its genesis through to successful delivery. It's also an easy and graceful way to move forward in life.

So let's say I had a light bulb moment to write a book and it got the green light from my gut and my heart fell in love with it, we can use the tenets of the eightfold path to help us move it forward.

The eightfold path

The right view

It is important that you have clarity in your vision and that you think through its whole life cycle, from creation to maturity and even through to its replacement and obsolescence.

The right resolve

We must hold our vision in our heart and see any rocky moments as opportunities for learning and improvement. Any serendipities that come our way are signs that we are on the right path. It pays dividends to thank them for coming along.

The right speech

In business, it is good karma to market your products and services by extolling their virtues and benefits and not by disparaging those of your competitors.

The right conduct

Act ethically and morally at all times. Bear the ecology of the planet in mind when using resources.

The right livelihood

Avoid being greedy and overambitious. Make some aspect of your products and services available to all, irrespective of how much they can afford.

The right effort

Work hard but don't work yourself into the ground. Take breaks but be fully focused when you are 'at work'.

The right mindfulness

Be constantly aware of your thoughts and feelings, their source and their purpose.

The right concentration

This simply means, at the very minimum, to take ten minutes of 'me time' each day.

I think you will agree that these eight concepts are both useful and practical. Follow them, and bear them in mind, and you will be successful in your endeavours.

Just Illuminate

With the eighth of these guidelines in mind, it is a good time to listen to the visualisation that accompanies this chapter. Here you will learn how to move your consciousness and awareness from the outer cortex of your brain, where it usually hangs out, to the pineal gland at the centre of your brain. From there you will be open to receive. When you do get an illumination, be sure to follow the framework at the end of this chapter to bring your ideas and innovations to successful fruition.

Key takeaways

The brain is both a generator and a receiver of thought.

Meditation allows us to tap into light bulb moments on demand.

Light bulb moments are whole mind events.

We make better decisions when our head, heart and gut are in agreement.

Follow the Noble Eightfold Path to make sure your good ideas actually happen.

Timing: being in time and on time

Timing has always been a key element in my life. I have been blessed to have been in the right place at the right time.

Buzz Aldrin

Timing: being in time and on time

In the last chapter, we explored one of my favourite mechanisms for saving time and that's to have a brilliant idea in 'no time at all'.

We also explored earlier how our efficiency drops when our attention wanders. Mindfulness meditation is a practical tool for management of our time.

We don't tend to give this much thought but seconds, minutes, hours, weeks and months don't exist in nature. Humankind have made them up to help run our modern-day society. Being able to measure and run to a standardised time system is great for meeting on time and catching a train on time. We don't want all planes to arrive at the same time at an airport, for example.

Go back just a few hundred years and nobody wore a watch. Now we have them on our wrists, our phones and our computers and we have clocks in most rooms in our house. Only Las Vegas casinos are clock-free zones so people lose track of both time and their wallets. In our modern day, 24x7, 'always on' society, our own time systems have unwittingly enslaved many of us. We have entrapped ourselves in a time system of our own making.

Our obsession with time has resulted in our language becoming littered with temporal references:

- 'Give me a second.'
- 'Just a minute.'
- 'Cometh the hour, cometh the man.'
- 'Clocking in late; clocking off early.'
- 'That is so last season.'
- 'Holding back the years.'

The subjectivity of time

As you listen to the meditative visualisations that accompany this book, you may notice that you lose track of time. Even though they are all exactly ten minutes long, you may experience time taking on an ethereal and 'stretchy' quality. The reason this happens is not so much because you imagine it, but because the flow of time itself alters for you personally.

If you have been waiting for a delayed plane at the end of a holiday, having read all your books, you will notice that time can stretch to eternity. Busy weekends with friends can just whizz by. Despite our amazing ability to measure time to fractions of a second, our personal experience of time is both subjective and variable.

One of the reasons for this is that the two halves of our brain experience time in different ways. It transpires that our left brain primarily sits inside space and time and our right brain sits everywhere and 'everywhen' else. So as you listen to the meditations, I use specific language patterns that activate both halves of the brain and help to induce the whole brain state. In addition, the background music I use puts slightly different signals into each ear, and thus each respective hemisphere, which also helps to harmonise the whole brain.

If somebody classically is called right-brained, they are said to be dreamy and to have their head in the clouds. As a result, they tend not to get things done. Someone who is left-brained, with eyes on the detail, can end up procrastinating and delay making any decisions until more analysis is carried out. Entering the whole brain state is the antidote to such 'stickiness'.

The breath clock

While some excellent research has been undertaken on bio-chemical and circadian clocks in our body and neurology, there is a fundamental clock in operation of which we are largely un-aware. It is the clock of our breath.

The life expectancy of a giant tortoise is around 120 to 140 years, and an elephant lives for around 80 to 90 years. While our life expectancy is increasing, in the Western world at least, go back 150 years and it was between 50 and 60 years. Now here's the thing: a tortoise breathes around four times every minute. An elephant breathes around eight times every minute. And we breathe around 12 to 15 times every minute. A mouse, by way of comparison, breaths 100 times a minute and lives only a couple of years.

So one of the best ways to change our relationship with time is to breathe more slowly. A positive spin-off from breathing more slowly is thought to be that it increases our longevity. To learn to do this, we need to use our diaphragm and to do belly breaths. This, of course, is how a baby breathes. We've just got out of the habit, as most of us breathe shallowly using only the inter-costal muscles around our ribs.

Now, you don't have to do it all the time, but just doing seven to nine deep and slow breaths at the start of the day is enough to slow things down. You can also do it before any creative task or if you are stressed. It works especially well if you are running late for a meeting. By breathing more slowly, we 'expand' time.

When we speak, we normally vocalise on the out breath. It is therefore the speed of our breath that gives rise to the speed at which we communicate. Such external communication is mirrored inside our heads in the form of 'self-talk'.

We don't often give this much of a thought, but the speed at which we talk to ourselves is around the speed that we talk out loud. The speed of thought, and talk, which is linked to the speed of our breath, gives rise to our sense of the passage of time. What's even more magical is that this technique works in groups, too, or when working one to one with clients, and it costs nothing to try.

So, it is only when we learn to talk and become self-aware, from around the age of three through to age seven, that our personal time clock really begins to tick. By using mindful meditative techniques, we 'un-learn' automatic 'self-talk' and retake control of our personal time machine.

So the key to creating more hours in each waking day lies in starting the day in the meditative state and maintaining it for as long as possible. When we practice mindfulness meditation regularly, we find that time stretches and that it distorts in a non-linear fashion. Allocated tasks seem to get done in the time slots available.

With practice, we can stay in the meditative state with our eyes open and keep our internal dialogue to a minimum. When we combine this practice with the utilisation of both left and right hemispheres, at the same time, our productivity increases by at least 200 per cent. I refer to this state as EMT – or Extended Me Time.

Going with the temporal flow

At the same time we created seconds, minutes and hours to sub-divide our days, we also created complex calendars to sub-divide our years. Again we don't give this much thought, but days of the week and the months of the year, with their unequal lengths, are all man-made. We have become enslaved by them, too.

We look forward to weekends, or week-ends, but never give any thought to week-starts. We set equal sales targets for each month when we know that the month of February is 10 per cent shorter than other months and some months are littered with bank holidays.

Our calendars, and the ubiquity of electric lighting, have made us lose complete track of real and natural time. All plants and all but domestic animals run to a completely different 'calendar' system. On planet earth, there are only three natural time constants and they are: the rotation of the earth on its axis (our days); the orbit of the moon around the earth (real months or moonths); and the orbit of the earth around the sun (our years). As the earth is inclined on its axis, our years give rise to the four seasons we call spring, summer, autumn and winter.

When we are mindful about natural time constants, we can begin to go with the temporal flow and stop pushing water uphill. For example, I discovered a few years ago that when I synchronised my projects with the moon phase, everything flowed with much more ease. This seems to work equally well for creative projects and for marketing initiatives. I also found that workshops timed for the new and full moons filled more easily, and that book launches on the new moon seem to be particularly successful.

We can also work in tune with the seasons. Only after writing three books did I notice that I'd started them all in spring. Springing forward and falling back is the way I now manage my years.

So, every spring there will be a major new initiative leading to a new harvest at the end of summer, just before Fall. I use the autumn and winter seasons to research and plan what will be unleashed at the start of the next spring. If you are someone who pays attention to detail, as I do, you can use the dates of the spring and autumn equinoxes and the winter and summer solstices to launch various activities.

Now, if this all sounds a bit pagan, then perhaps our ancestors knew of a simpler way to run their lives. Unlike our ancestors, we don't have to buy into any superstitions or dogma, but just roll with the seasons. Like many of the techniques in this book, it costs nothing to try, and there's an upside to being mindful of all of our planning and timing.

Just in time

When we re-synchronise our activities with natural time, something rather magical happens. External events start to turn up just at the right time. If we were to track back in time to when life was a struggle, we can see that all that was happening was that we were trying to do something at a non-optimal time. Conversely, when we were in flow, we had been perhaps unconsciously in sync with the natural times of year.

Just a Moment

The visualisation that accompanies this chapter is a real treat. It encourages the listener to pay attention to and savour each of the moments that fill our waking days which, together, create our lives. I hope by now you are appreciating that these ten minute visualisations do not so much require you to spend time listening to them, but that they are actually an investment in time. Time is merely a consensual illusion that helps us to experience what we call reality. It's also handy as it stops everything from happening all at once.

Key takeaways

The passage of time is subjective.

The speed of our breath affects the perceived flow of time.

We have become enslaved by our man-made time systems.

We have lost touch with natural time.

When we go with the flow, events start to happen 'just in time'.

I must govern the clock, not be governed by it.

Golda Meir

Allowing: getting opportunities to come to you

Creativity is allowing yourself to make mistakes. Art is knowing which ones to keep.

Scott Adams

Allowing: getting opportunities to come to you

When we become accustomed to the most perfect events turning up 'just in time', we open the door to a new way of being. The most perfect opportunities find us, without the need to seek them out.

A good example of this phenomenon is this book itself. I had no plans to write it at all this year. It came from a conversation with the publisher about interviewing authors for my podcast. We ended up talking about ideas for another book in the Authority Guide series. I checked in with my heart and my gut before I allowed my head to make the decision to go ahead. I wrote it speedily, and I hope effectively, by entering the EMT state.

When we allow the most perfect events to land at our door, it's an easier and less stressful way to be. By focusing our attention on the task in hand, entering the EMT state and engaging our whole brain creatively, we already get a boost in productivity. This leads to another benefit. When we entrust that external events are conspiring with us, not against us, we can apply even more focus to what we are doing right at this moment in time. We become comfortable and safe in the knowledge that 'things will just turn up'.

On the surface, this might sound like a naive and falsely optimistic way to be. When you experience it happening to you, as most people have at some time or other, it is transformative. Like all new ways to be, it takes a little trust and practice. You will experience false dawns and, if you are like me, can get overexcited by the early wins. The dividends to be earned are amazing and, like any investment portfolio, it pays to repeat and reinvest in what works well.

Mindful listening

You may have heard the adage that we have two ears and one mouth and that we should use them in this proportion. If we are either talking or self-talking, it is virtually impossible to listen. The sights and sounds that are around us are what we use to inform ourselves of what is occurring. In business, it is important to listen to what our employees, our boss, our suppliers and our customers are saying. We should be mindful, too, of what their body language is saying when we are with them. Furthermore, we should also be mindful of what is not being said. There may be a reason that clients are not calling or visiting your website.

While we should be paying attention to conversations going on around us, we should also be mindful of our internal self-talk.

Some years ago, some neuroscientists noticed something strange happening with subjects in MRI scanners. If they were presented with a stimulus, such as a flashing image, some of the neurons in the gut mind seemed to fire quite a few seconds before the stimulus was presented.

Our gut, or enteric mind, sits between the outer muscle wall in our colon and the inner digestive tract. In humans, the gut mind contains more neurons than are in a cat's brain. Although it may sound a bit bizarre, it transpires that we have areas in our neurology that work ahead of time.

Becoming an ultrapreneur

The word entrepreneur comes from the old French word *entre-prendre* meaning 'to undertake'. It's thought that it has even earlier roots in the Sanskrit phrase of *Antha Prerna*, which means 'self-motivated'.

It's unquestionable, entrepreneurs have to be 'self-motivated' and they have to 'undertake' all manner of things. Entrepreneurs are human, too, and suffer bouts of self-doubt and sometimes fall on hard times. Each entrepreneur has an angel on one shoulder driving them forward. On the other sits a devil telling them not to be so silly and to go and get a day job.

The most successful entrepreneurs are focused on doing exactly the right things, in the right order, right now. Even blessed with these basic temporal powers, they have that other trick up their sleeve. They can jump outside time itself by tapping into light bulb moments on demand. This allows them to get the whole picture for the most amazing ideas in less than a split second.

We can think of an entrepreneur who goes along with the flow of time as being an 'ultrapreneur'. Their secret is this. The ease with which they generate ideas, and make things happen, is because they are always a few seconds ahead of everyone else. When an ultrapreneur is on fire, everyone else is playing catch-up.

We can have some linguistic fun with this new pseudo-word.

Ultrapreneur (noun): an entrepreneur who is way ahead of the pack. [Derivation: ultra- (Latin: beyond) and -preneur (French: prendre, to take)]

What separates those who make it from those who struggle is mindset. This is not as trivial as holding an optimistic 'glass half full' mentality in the face of adversity. In fact, the most

Allowing: getting opportunities to come to you

successful entrepreneurs positively thrive in the face of adversity. When they struggle over something, or see others having a hard time, they know that if they come up with a solution to solve this problem, they will be on to a winner. Especially, too, if that winner saves or makes those who invest in it more than it costs them.

The most successful ultrapreneurs are the ones who positively thrive when the wheels come off the bus and life throws them a curved ball.

Dealing with curved balls

You may find it is relatively easy to be 'in the zone', and EMT, when you are by yourself, but when you meet with others, their time clocks might be running at different rates, which can throw yours out of kilter.

Employers, fellow workers, family members, kids and even pets have temporal needs of their own that can throw you out of your extended time perspective into a more frenetic world. If this happens, there are some simple techniques you can employ to minimise the disruption. They take a little practice, discipline and trust, and require you to be 'insight-full' about what happens when you encounter such interruptions.

The first aspect of being thrown out of EMT is to realise that your train of thought has been disrupted. When you had been 'in the zone', your internal dialogue has now taken a new course, which incorporates aspects of someone else's world and thought flow. If the disruption is severe, it might stir up thought forms of anger, despair, fear or hurt from your lower mind centres, and any thought of creativity flies out of the window. You can enter a 'mindfall' of someone else's making.

When this happens, and you feel events need your immediate attention, and before you dive into an alternate time frame, take three deep in and out breaths. If nothing else, this will steel you for what is about to unfold. If you find you have to drop everything, wrap up what you are doing and be thankful for the interruption – it might be a blessing in disguise.

If the interruption is severe, say like a family illness or a problem in business that diverts production resources, there may also be an underlying message. The illness could be a cry for help and an early warning of something that needs immediate treatment. Or something may need to be fixed in the business so that a bigger problem doesn't appear down the line.

In all adversity lies opportunity and it is worth reflecting on the four modes of mindfulness and what our body, our feelings, our thoughts and the 'way of things' might tell us.

An attitude of gratitude

If you were to record all the thoughts in your head over a particular day and play them back to yourself, it might prove to be quite an excruciating exercise. You'd hear yourself commenting on people and events that you come across, rehearsing things you plan to say and replaying conversations you have had. You might have some random and creative thoughts. Almost certainly in the mix will be some thoughts of worry, fear and perhaps even anger.

Our conscious mind only holds one thought at a time. It selects that thought from millions, if not billions, of possible thought forms that can be instigated through external events that impinge on our senses, and impressions that percolate up from our lower mind centres. Other thought forms from the collective mind can also sneak their way in.

One analogy that is often used is that our conscious mind is like the rider on an elephant, where the elephant represents our unconscious mind. For some of the time, the rider is able to steer the elephant, but if the elephant wants to wander off on its own, the rider will be helpless to stop it. I am sure, like me, you have experienced this happening.

If the rider is holding the fear of being out of control, the elephant will be uncontrollable. If the rider is angry, they can find themselves on top of a raging bull of an elephant.

A great way to make the rider stronger, and the elephant more controllable, is to adopt the attitude of gratitude. If we awaken and hold the thought of gratitude in our heads for the duration of the day, it helps us to see everything that comes our way as just perfect, and arriving just when we need it. We end up becoming grateful for both interruptions and those curved balls.

Just for Tomorrow

What we do today sets up the conditions for what unfolds tomorrow. This next meditation can be done any time of the day but you might find it works well if listened to in the evening, or just before you go to bed. If you do listen to it in bed and fall asleep, it still works.

Key takeaways

Allowing is the secret to becoming lucky in business.

It pays dividends to really listen.

Ultrapreneurs are ahead of everyone else.

From time to time, curved balls will come our way but always carry a message.

An attitude of gratitude will smooth the path.

Collaborating: using mindfulness in teams

That's the nice thing about collaborating with someone: Your work becomes a conversation.

Noah Baumbach

Collaborating: using mindfulness in teams

A journey into the world of mindfulness is a personal choice and a personal exploration. It is not for everyone.

My hope is that you enjoy the short journey together through this book and that you will continue your explorations further. When we love what we do, it's natural we want to share that love and help others too. We have to be mindful, though, that everyone is on their own path and journey and at different stages of development.

So if you own a business, or are a manager in a business, and you want to introduce mindfulness into the business, getting everyone in a room on a dress-down Friday afternoon chanting 'Omm' is not the optimum way to go about it. For starters, everyone's mind will be gravitating to what they are doing that weekend and wondering if they can finish early to avoid the rush hour.

Teaching mindfulness in the workplace might not be the ideal environment either as noises and distractions abound. A stealth-full approach has to be taken.

Breathing together

The breath is much more powerful than even this book has implied. It drives everything. The speed of our breath affects the perceived passage of time. Everything that is alive breathes, too. Plants, insects and aquatic lifeforms don't have lungs as such but exchange gases in order to stay alive. The earth's surface 'breathes' as the moon passes around it causing winds and tides on the surface and stirring up tectonic motion beneath the crust and in the core. The sun cycles light from its core to the surface in massive eddies and magnetic whirlpools. Everything is in cyclical motion.

Coming back down to earth, and into the boardroom, we can put this esoteric knowledge to good and practical use. Either in a one-to-one meeting or a meeting with several people, if you slow your breathing down mindfully, everyone will track you. When you speak, speaking slowly and methodically will cause others to speak less quickly and excitedly. Try it for some fun and you will be amazed how quickly it works.

Now that you are mindful about the role of the breath, you will spot two spin-off benefits. The first is that more creativity will flow as people are more in-spired. Second, the speed of time will slow down for everyone, so more is achieved in the meeting.

Once you have tried this in stealth mode, you can then let some people in on the secret. Let's say you try it first with a meeting with one person or a handful of people and you then want to scale it up to a hundred or so. What you will need to do is to involve some colleagues and get them to follow your lead and breathe at the same rate as you. If you accentuate the rise and fall of your stomach, they will be able to track you. If you are speaking, they will know when you are breathing out as we speak on the out breath.

Note that when controlling others covertly in this manner, it is crucial that you only hold everyone's highest good in mind. If you work in a more enlightened environment, you can be less covert and more overt about all of this. For example, before a creative meeting, you can take the whole team through the nostril breathing exercise to get everyone's whole brain activated. Collective diaphragmatic breathing can be used as well, to synchronise and slow down the collective speed of time.

Mindful mails

As part and parcel of becoming mindful about our personal time management, we have to respect how our actions and behaviours impact on the time of others. So rather than interrupting someone when they are obviously tied up and busy, wait for an appropriate gap in their attention.

Another huge collective time waster is email. Make sure just one person is in the To field and only those who need to be are in the Cc field. Invoking the Bcc field can be a time waster, too, potentially causing someone who shouldn't have seen the email to drop you or themselves in it by unwittingly 'Replying to All'. Just send them a forwarded version marked 'For their eyes and information only'.

Aside from such nuances in protocol, just sending and replying to less emails collectively, dramatically saves time for everyone. Get into the habit of checking emails first thing, in the middle of the day and at the end of the day. Try to have weekends off and see whether you can spread this change around your organisation. As soon as people know you won't reply at the weekend, it is amazing how quickly they stop sending you emails.

Seeing and agreeing together

Running an effective meeting is both an art and a science. The meeting chairperson, or facilitator, should be mindful of the time commitment of all attendees. Likewise, the attendees should arrive on time and prepared, thus respecting the time of all the other attendees.

For strategic, creative and planning meetings, an agenda is useful as is an agreed framework for the meeting. In creative meetings, I love using tools like Edward de Bono's Six Thinking Hats or Appreciative Inquiry. With De Bono's Six Thinking Hats, you look at an idea or a problem from six different standpoints. With Appreciative Inquiry, you take something as it exists with all its good and bad attributes and simply focus on making it better. Both are examples of parallel thinking.

More recently, I have been hosting meetings using a collective Mind Map to which everyone contributes. A simple example I use for onward development of an idea or a product is one I call the Four A's (Figure 5). It has four branches and you start top right and go around the map in a clockwise direction.

Figure 5 The Four A's

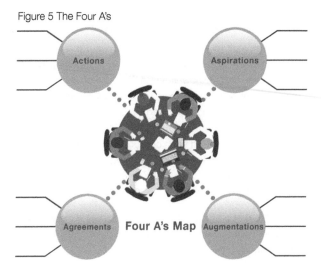

First you capture everyone's *aspirations*. Ask what they would like to achieve by making the change.

Next you elicit what would have to be *augmented* in order to fulfil those aspirations.

Third, list all the points that the attendees *agree* on.

Lastly, allocate *actions* to take you closer to the aspirations. This might involve some people doing some research before the follow-on meeting.

Now this might sound simple, because it is, but be mindful how everything is designed to bring consensus and move things for-ward. There is no space for navel gazing or negativity. This map, by the way, can also be used on yourself, either to help with a personal issue or to shed light on a project.

Harnessing the group mind

Some meetings might be less straightforward than a product planning meeting, as described above. There may be imponderables and unknowns and differences of opinion. Some people might be in two or more minds about something. Some attendees' right brains might hold the vision but their left brains have yet to fill in the detail. The person who is underwriting the project might have a left brain consumed by mounting costs on a spreadsheet and a right brain that has not yet grasped the vision. For them, no action is the action to be taken, which is frustrating for the visionaries.

Herding a group of cats of this nature requires a more cunning approach, where everyone's opinions are valued, respected and taken into account.

For any meeting to reach full consensus, it is vital that the heads, hearts and gut minds of all attendees are in agreement. Otherwise what happens is that some people reluctantly agree and then begrudgingly drag their feet or throw toys out of the pram, and generally make things difficult post-meeting.

So the meeting facilitator can ask everyone in turn if their gut gives the project a green or a red light. If there are any red lights, then ask what would have to change to turn the light green. Debate all red lights until you get all greens.

Next, once the lights are all green, ask everyone if, in their heart of hearts, they love the idea or are lukewarm or positively cold about it. Again ask what would have to change for them to fall in love with the idea.

Once you are close to a 'group hug', it's time to engage all right brains and elicit all the blue sky ideas for the project. Find out whether everyone sees the big picture of where this could go.

Next engage the collective left brains and iron out all the detail required to make the project into a reality.

This process is very similar to the Four A's map, De Bono's Six Thinking Hats and Appreciative Enquiry. Where it differs subtly is that it is mindful of the different mind centres that we often unconsciously access to make better decisions.

Bringing what we are unconscious of into our conscious awareness is one of the most beautiful outputs from mindfulness meditation. So if you use any of the techniques above and people admire you for their efficacy, the biggest service you can give is to share the secret, which they in turn will share with others.

Collective thoughts

There is an old saying that the family that prays together, stays together. In these secular and multi-faith days, it is probably not a good idea to call the workforce to morning prayers. We can, however, instil an atmosphere and culture of collective thinking. Ideally, for some of the time, this will involve teams thinking the same way and focusing on the same goals.

Where mindfulness in the workplace really comes to the fore is when we respect and encourage differences in ways of thinking. Two or more brains are definitely better than the two halves of our own brain.

By introducing a culture of mindfulness into the workplace, we create more time for everyone. The resulting culture of time-fulness leads us to a place where we can be kinder to each other and to ourselves. This leads us to the state of kindfulness. Being mindful, timeful and kindful at the same time leads us collectively to a better world.

Just Imagine

The world that we imagine today has the tendency to be the world that we live in tomorrow. This next visualisation connects you with that world so that you can take small steps today for it to become your reality.

Key takeaways

The breath has collective power.

Respect the time of others as if it's your own.

The team that sees and agrees together will stay together.

Harness the power of the group mind.

What we imagine today becomes the world we live in tomorrow.

Lovingness: loving the work that you do

You never lose by loving. You always lose
by holding back.

Barbara de Angelis

Lovingness: loving the work that you do

You will have heard it said that when we love the work that we do, we will never work again.

By collaborating creatively, the voices of the whole team get heard. People love to be listened to and respected. This is the precursor to operating at a whole new level.

Now, work itself is a word that we associate with something that is unpleasant, which we have to do just to pay the bills and keep the wolf from the door. Work implies that effort must be used. Some people are correspondingly 'work-shy'. Conversely, love is a word that can often be misused. Some people might use the word love when they merely like something. In the early stages of a relationship, we might be more in lust than in love.

The word love comes up pretty much constantly in our culture. You cannot listen to an hour of popular music on the radio without at least one song being played that has love in the title or at least in its lyrics. Put the word love into an Amazon search, and you will find around half a million books with love in their titles or content. Love is definitely in the air, love is all around us and love is a drug, with addictive qualities.

Like the word 'nice', it can suffer somewhat from overuse. It is important to be mindful of our own use of the word so we only use it when we absolutely mean it. This is a word to be cherished and not one to be diluted. If people around us hear that we simply love everything, then they will not take us seriously when we really love something or someone. It is wise to make judicious choices between what we love and what we merely like. This holds true, too, for the use of the heart emoticon in our text and social media messages.

Words hold and transmit a power through the airwaves similar to thoughts in the field of the collective consciousness. So when we speak, either out loud or 'in loud', use the word love sparingly, and mindfully, and when you really mean it.

Starting a to love list

To start living a life that you love, the first step to take is to switch from dreading the tasks on your to-do list and to reformulate them using a to love list. Just imagine if everything on your to-do list was something you simply loved to do.

We can get somewhat overwhelmed with our to-do lists. Some people have several of them that they just add to, so that they never get any shorter. As a result, like our email Inbox, they can get bigger and bigger and become completely unmanageable and unwieldy. Some people even spend so much time curating their to-do lists that they end up not getting anything done.

Here's how to create a to love list. You'll need two blank sheets of paper. Label one sheet of paper a to love list and one a to don't list.

First, scan all the items on your to-do list, or lists, and transfer the ones you would rather not do over to the sheet labelled to don't list. Cross them off your to-do list as you go. You should now be left with a to-do list with just the things you like doing. Next, in the order that you would love to do them, transfer them to the blank sheet of paper labelled as your to love list.

Now have a look at your to don't list. It will probably have things on it that need doing, even if you don't like to do them. See which ones you can outsource or delegate to someone else. Then take action to pass them on. With the tasks you have left, have a think of how you could tackle them or what would have to change so you would love to do them. Then move them across to your to love list.

At this point, you should be able to rip up the old to-do list and bin the to don't list. The next step is easy: just tackle your to love list from the top down. This way, you will only do the things you like doing the most in the order you'd love to do them. What's not to love about that?

Sharing the love

The love we share out, unconditionally, seems to bounce back to us, often amplified. There are some caveats to sharing love freely, though. Be mindful that some might not be ready or willing to receive it. Others might think you've joined a cult. The biggest caveat, however, is that you should be mindful not to deplete yourself of love.

Our heart centre is capable of sending out love, but it also needs to receive love. To maintain good health and wellbeing, in flow and out flow has to be balanced. When people are made redundant, or divorce, they can take this on board as a lack of love in their world and this can lead to heart and circulatory conditions.

The flow of love is not just in and out from our heart centre. Energy flows in our neurology up and down, too. If we speak or think less than loving words, by bad-mouthing people or things, the energy from our throat and head weakens our heart accordingly. Gossip around the water cooler or harbouring less than positive thoughts about people ultimately bounces back at us.

As Buddha said, 'Holding on to anger is like holding a hot coal and not throwing it.' If we are not grounded in what we do or ignore our intuitions from our lower mind centres, the heart 'feels' undervalued and suffers. When it comes to being heart-full, we should be mind-full about how we go about it.

Just as for ideas, loving what you do is a whole mind activity. When people see you loving what you do, you become attractive. Colleagues, suppliers and clients love working with you and doing business with you. Selling becomes easier when people just want to share time with you and buy a piece of you.

Just Love

This visualisation extends the concept first introduced when moving consciousness from the outer cortex to the pineal gland. With a little practice, and mind-full-ness, we can move our awareness to anywhere in our body, and anywhere outside our body, too. For example, you can become aware of your big toe right now. So imagine what it's like to be inside a big toe and sharing a sock with some other toes. We can not only move our consciousness to our heart centre but also, with a little practice, let it reside there. This visualisation takes you there and activates some dormant and nascent qualities of the heart.

Key takeaways

We should aim to love the work we do.

The words we use contain power as well as meaning.

It's time to ditch our to-do lists and switch to a to love list.

Loving what we do is essential for our wellbeing.

It's important we share the love mindfully.

Ending: the start of a new way of being

The good life is one inspired by love and guided by knowledge.

Bertrand Russell

Ending: the start of a new way of being

So we come to the end of this short journey exploring some aspects of practical mindfulness. I hope you have picked up some useful information and some tips and techniques that will serve you well in your onward journey.

This book is mindfully short and brief while, at the same time, being wide and deep in some of the concepts it has introduced. When we come to the end of one thing, it neatly brings us to a new beginning of something else. My hope is that you discover that indulging in ten minutes of daily 'me time' brings you untold benefits and leads you to a new way of being.

New beginnings

To usher in new ways to be, it helps if we take the opportunity to allow old habits and patterns that don't serve us to slip away at the same time. I am a big fan of win–win situations. A great way to begin this process is to find something you want to stop doing for ten minutes and to use that time for your daily meditation. Try not opening emails first thing and replying to them, for example.

Now you appreciate the singular nature of thought, try replacing repetitive thought patterns with thoughts of creativity. Ask the thoughts that you don't want around to go away and notice how this leaves space for new thoughts to arrive.

When you are short of ideas, just breathe. If your creativity runs dry, power your hemispheres with a few nostril breaths or go for a walk. The time you take out will easily come back to you. When you take your foot off the throttle, you will quickly gather momentum again when you return to the task in hand.

When you start to benefit from this new approach, you can scale up these benefits by sharing your secrets with those around you. Lead by example and without preaching. Be mindful of how you impact upon the time and attention of others and be firm when they impact upon your time.

Just Be

To bring this part of your journey to a close, I would like to leave you with a visualisation that will open many new doors and take you down some unimaginable paths. Travel safely, take it slow and steady and above all be mindful, timeful and kindful about how you go about your days.

For the next ten days after reading this book, listen to any of the visualisations that accompany this book again, in any order that takes your heart's fancy, and allow a new world to arrive at your doorstep.

This last visualisation uses the idea behind the Just Imagine visualisation and takes it up a notch. Just imagine that there is a world out there which is beyond your imagination. You can't right? If we can't imagine something, then even if you are fabulous at creating and manifesting your world, it is hard to conjure it into existence. The only way to step into this even brighter world is to allow it to come to you.

Resources

For more on how to tap into unlimited inspiration, read *The Art and Science of Light Bulb Moments* (Evans, T. (2011) O Books).

Managing Time Mindfully (Evans, T. (2015) Tmesis Ltd) is a temporal exploration that will change your relationship with the clock.

To live a mindful existence where serendipity visits your door daily, read *Mindful Timeful Kindful* (Evans, T. (2015) Tmesis Ltd).

To get in and stay in your creative flow, read *The Zone: How to Get in It and Stay in It* (Evans, T. (2014) Tmesis Ltd).

To find out how an ex-BBC TV engineer unexpectedly became a meditation guide without ever visiting an ashram, read *New Magic for a New Era* (Evans, T. (2015) Tmesis Ltd).

You will find a full list of all Tom's books here: www.tomevans. co/books

In addition, Tom has created hours of self-study materials for those looking to deepen their appreciation of the applications of practical mindfulness: www.tomevans.co/newmagic

About the author

Tom Evans is an ex-BBC TV engineer who became an author by accident in his mid-40s, after discovering how to meditate. These days, he invests his time writing, and inspiring, teaching and running several philanthropic initiatives. He is an engaging and edutaining speaker and workshop host.

He is also the host of the popular Zone Show podcast. He is a meditation guide on the world's most downloaded free meditation app, Insight Timer, and he has created the world's first time management programme based on mindfulness, called Living Timefully.

He still doesn't know what he wants to be when he grows up.

Find out more at www.tomevans.co

Follow him on Twitter at www.twitter.com/thebookwright

Listen to the Zone Show podcast at www.thezoneshow.com